Nutrition

Fats

by Sue Bradford Edwards

FOCUS READERS

BEACON

www.focusreaders.com

Focus Readers is distributed by North Star Editions:
sales@northstareditions.com | 888-417-0195

Produced for Focus Readers by Red Line Editorial.

Photographs ©: Shutterstock Images, cover, 1, 4, 7, 8, 10, 13, 14–15, 16, 19, 20, 22, 25, 27, 29

Library of Congress Cataloging-in-Publication Data
Names: Edwards, Sue Bradford, author.
Title: Fats / by Sue Bradford Edwards.
Description: Mendota Heights, MN: Focus Readers, [2025] | Series: Nutrition | Includes index. | Audience: Grades 2-3
Identifiers: LCCN 2023053411 (print) | LCCN 2023053412 (ebook) | ISBN 9798889981824 (hardcover) | ISBN 9798889982388 (paperback) | ISBN 9798889983484 (pdf) | ISBN 9798889982944 (ebook)
Subjects: LCSH: Fatty acids in human nutrition--Juvenile literature. | Fat--Juvenile literature. | Nutrition--Juvenile literature.
Classification: LCC QP752.F35 E393 2025 (print) | LCC QP752.F35 (ebook) | DDC 612.3/97--dc23/eng/20231229
LC record available at https://lccn.loc.gov/2023053411
LC ebook record available at https://lccn.loc.gov/2023053412

Printed in the United States of America
Mankato, MN
082024

About the Author

Sue Bradford Edwards lives in St. Louis, Missouri. She writes nonfiction for young readers. Her books include *Investigating Fossil Fuel Pollution, Haunted History of San Antonio and the Alamo, Stem Cells, Puggle: Pugs Meet Beagles!*, and *Labradoodle: Labrador Retrievers Meet Poodles!*

Table of Contents

Chapter 1

Making Breakfast

A boy and his mother make breakfast together. The boy's mom pours olive oil into a pan. Then she cracks open a few eggs and scrambles them.

Nearly all of the fats in eggs are found in the yolk.

Next, the boy grabs an avocado. His mom cuts it up. They scoop the scrambled eggs and avocado onto tortillas. Then, the boy rolls them up. Eggs, avocados, and olive oil are three healthy sources of fat.

While the boy finishes the wraps, his mom puts strawberries and water into a blender. She also adds

Many people think fats are bad to eat. But some kinds are important for health.

Up to 35 percent of the body's energy comes from fats.

chia seeds. The seeds are another source of healthy fat. She blends the **ingredients** together.

The boy and his mother eat their breakfast. The meal gives them plenty of energy for the morning.

Chapter 2

Healthy Fats

When a person eats fat, the body breaks it down. The fat turns into fatty acids. Blood moves fatty acids around the body. The body may use fatty acids for energy. Or it may use them to build new fats.

The body uses some fats right away. Other fatty acids are stored.

Fish such as salmon have essential fatty acids. Fatty acids are good for people's skin and bones.

The human body can make some fats. But other kinds must come from food. These types are called essential fatty acids.

Fats help the body store energy. Then, the body can use the

energy when it is needed. Fats also help the body use **vitamins** and **minerals**.

Fats are found throughout the body. They protect organs. Fats also make up **cell membranes**. Cell membranes let helpful things pass through cells. They keep harmful things out.

Fats do other things. They make food taste good. They also help people feel full. That way, people know when to stop eating.

Foods contain different types of fat. Unsaturated fats are important for good health. These kinds of fats are liquid at room temperature.

Other fats are unhealthy. These fats are usually solid at room temperature. Trans fats are one example. They can cause **inflammation**. That can lead to

Fats are very important for young children. They help the body grow.

Some trans fats form naturally in animals. Trans fats can be found in certain meats, such as beef.

heart disease or **diabetes**. Even small amounts of trans fats are unhealthy.

Saturated fats cause less harm than trans fats. They can be eaten in small amounts. But larger amounts can be unhealthy.

A CLOSER LOOK

Omega-3s

Omega-3 fatty acids keep the brain and heart healthy. They help stop **blood clots** from forming. The body can make some omega-3 fatty acids. The body starts with one type of omega-3. Then, it uses that fatty acid to build another type. But the body cannot make enough of these fatty acids. So, people must get omega-3s from food. These foods include flaxseeds and walnuts. Fish is another good source. People should try to eat foods with omega-3s every day.

Omega-3s are important for babies' brains and vision.

Chapter 3

Many Options

Fats are found in many foods. The healthiest fats are unsaturated fats. These fats can be split into two groups. The first is monounsaturated fats. They are found in olive oil and avocados.

Unsaturated fats are important for heart health.

Many nuts and seeds have monounsaturated fats, too. These include almonds and pecans. Pumpkin seeds and sesame seeds also have them.

The second kind of healthy fats are called polyunsaturated fats. Omega-3 fats are one example. Another type is omega-6 fats. Omega-6 fats are found in soybeans. They are also in eggs.

Saturated fats are healthy only in small amounts. These fats are

Experts suggest that people get less than 10 percent of calories from saturated fats.

found in meat. Red meats, such as beef and pork, have the most. But poultry products, such as chicken and duck, have some, too.

Trans fats may form when oil is cooked at high heat.

Many dairy foods have high levels of saturated fats. These foods include butter and cheese. Certain oils also have lots of saturated fats. Examples include palm oil and coconut oil.

Trans fats are unhealthy even in small amounts. Store-bought baked goods may have trans fats. These include cookies and cakes.

Trans fats may also be in fried foods. French fries and donuts are two examples. Snacks such as microwave popcorn may also have high levels. So can frozen pizza.

Added trans fats are illegal in many countries. But they can still be found in many parts of the world.

Chapter 4

Choosing Fats

People need fats. But it is important to choose healthy sources. Experts suggest that people do not avoid all fats. Instead, they should focus on eating more unsaturated fats.

Guacamole is made with avocados. It is a good source of unsaturated fat.

Often, people can substitute healthy fats for unhealthy fats. For example, people can cook food with olive oil instead of butter. They can eat fish instead of red meat. For snacks, they can eat nuts and seeds instead of potato chips.

There are other ways to eat more healthy fats. People can avoid **processed** foods. These foods often have added fats. Added fats can make foods taste good. But they are unhealthy for the body. Processed

Processed foods tend to have high levels of saturated and trans fats.

foods include some meats. Hot dogs and lunch meats are two examples. Many sweet foods are also processed. Cakes and cookies often have unhealthy fats. Sugary breakfast cereals do, too.

People should eat **whole foods** instead of processed foods. Avocados and eggs are good choices. Yogurts with low amounts of added sugar are another healthy option.

Experts also suggest eating foods with omega-3s every day. One way to get more omega-3s is

People can check for unhealthy fats. Reading food labels helps.

Fish oil supplements can help people get more omega-3s.

to eat fish. Salmon and mackerel are good choices. So are anchovies and herring. Plant-based foods can also help. Chia seeds and brussels sprouts are good options.

FOCUS ON

Fats

Write your answers on a separate piece of paper.

1. Write a sentence describing the main ideas of Chapter 4.
2. What is your favorite source of unsaturated fat? Why?
3. What kind of fats are unhealthy in any amount?
   - A. unsaturated fats
   - B. trans fats
   - C. saturated fats
4. What might happen if a person did not eat enough omega-3s?
   - A. She would be able to store more energy.
   - B. She would feel less tired.
   - C. She would be more likely to get blood clots.

5. What does **products** mean in this book?

*These fats are found in meat. Red meats, such as beef and pork, have the most. But poultry **products**, such as chicken and duck, have some, too.*

A. foods with lots of fat
B. healthy foods
C. things people can buy

6. What does **substitute** mean in this book?

*Often, people can **substitute** healthy fats for unhealthy fats. For example, people can cook food with olive oil instead of butter.*

A. to use instead of something
B. to add more of something
C. to stop using something

Answer key on page 32.

Glossary

blood clots
Clumps of dried blood that can stop blood from flowing.

cell membranes
The thin walls that surround cells.

diabetes
A disease that affects how the body breaks down energy and blood sugar.

inflammation
Heat, redness, and swelling that are part of the body's response to disease.

ingredients
Foods that are mixed together to make a meal.

minerals
Substances found in food that come from soil or water.

processed
When food is changed by adding something to it or by preparing it in a certain way.

vitamins
Nutrients humans need to grow and stay healthy.

whole foods
Foods that have not been processed.

To Learn More

BOOKS

Nelson, Louise. *Healthy Eating*. Minneapolis: Jump!, 2024.

Rebman, Nick. *Earth-Friendly Eating.* Mendota Heights, MN: Focus Readers, 2022.

Ziemann, Kimberly. *Fats As Necessary Nutrients.* Minneapolis: Abdo Publishing, 2023.

NOTE TO EDUCATORS

Visit **www.focusreaders.com** to find lesson plans, activities, links, and other resources related to this title.

Index

Answer Key: 1. Answers will vary; **2.** Answers will vary; **3.** B; **4.** C; **5.** C; **6.** A